49030
C45

791.3 VIA

Véronique Vial

"Wings"

Backstage with

Cirque du Soleil !!!

Photographs by Véronique Vial

Préface by Guy Laliberté

TONDO

PREFACE

This book is the result of a fruitful encounter between Véronique Vial and Cirque du Soleil. While the initial purpose of the venture was to document certain facets of our shows, it soon gave rise to a unique photographic essay. On seeing the first prints, we immediately felt the impact of her work—Véronique has succeeded in portraying the intimacy of the artists' lives.

For the general public, this book unlocks the door to a secret universe: the back-stage area, where performers find the strength and energy they need to offer the best of themselves in performance. Millions of spectators have seen a Cirque du Soleil production, yet few have had the privilege of visiting this hallowed place. Véronique's camera opens up this universe to us.

Only an artist of Véronique's calibre could convey the essence of this magical world. Thanks to her unique sensitivity, she has been able to capture these moments that are so precious to us. Thank you, Véronique.

We continue to work together; Véronique will be immortalizing many more moments in the life of Cirque du Soleil. More importantly, however, our friend-ship has grown, and Véronique is now a part of our extended family.

Guy Laliberté
Founding President, Cirque du Soleil

FOREWORD

When I first saw Cirque du Soleil, I wanted to run away with them forever!!!

After meeting Guy Laliberté, the Founding President, we decided to try some photography backstage with the coordination and very special help of my friend Hélène Dufresne.

I have travelled with Cirque du Soleil for over five years throughout Canada, Europe and the United States, capturing the magic that follows them wherever they go— backstage, on stage, or at the "Cantina." The time that I have shared with all of the artists has been a visual feast and a permanent source of inspiration.

After spending time, like a fly on the wall, trying not to disturb their rehearsals, or their warming up, or the five minutes of rest they steal between acts, I've become very familiar with these wonderful artists. They come from everywhere and many different languages are spoken backstage which makes it even more exotic to communicate. There is a Cirque universal language in the "artistic tent" that is a visual one.

The "artistic tent" is where I shot most of the backstage photographs. The performers spend a lot of time backstage between their acts. In all of the various Cirque shows, including "New Experience," "Saltimbanco," "Quidam," and "Mystère," the artists created a big family of warmth and they always welcomed me.

Véronique Vial

Photographs

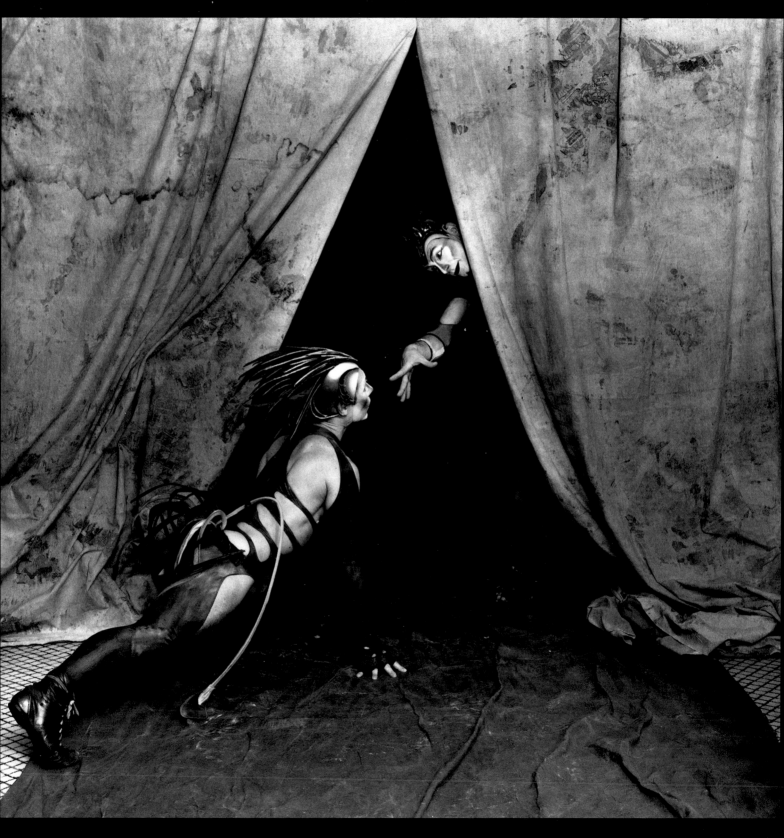

Le lézard vert et

son pivert de terre...!!!

Sous son chapeau

Dans les anneaux de l'escargot ...

le paon s'éventaille ...

brin d'Âme

Poudre d'Étoile

Dans les plis et replis . . . .

!!! Troubadour !!!

Des balades en tournade !!!

Fantôme Solitaire   . . .

Ruès Temporaines   . . .

L' élastique en fraîcheur

tique dans la blancheur . . . .

Il épie ... invisible

Sous sa cible ...!!!

!!! Agile !!!

La brindille qui aiguille ...

Fleurs des Isles

Oiseaux Sauvages

Sur le fils ....

lointain voyage

De leurs ficelles

elles ensorcellent   .!!!

Tout ce cordage n'encre

pas les rêves tenches !!

Elle s'avalanche ...

s'avalanche de sa cadence

La beauté du Corps se

réveille en décor !!!

L' "échauffement

d'un "faux semblant !!!

Envoûtée par les cordes

elle s'abandonne !!!

La communion de la

sueur, la chaire et l'habit ...

L'Ange noir s'enivre

du silence du jour !!!

L'envoûtement de la

princesse aux anneaux . . .

La contorsion

du paon !!!

Enveloppé par la corde

il se donne !!!

La corde commence son

rituel boatique . . . .

Un, deux, trois .... dix doigts

pour porter la terre !!!

La belle et la bête

. . . Emballées . . .

La detente du Hibous

... et sérieuse !!!

Ce grand nez, est pour mieux

vous sentir .... mon enfant !!!

Mesure, Cadence, mesure et cadence

Les Fliboux se balancent . . .

Fête Sauvage – du plumage

Échauffé, l'épervier

planifie sa volée ...

!!! Quel Trésor !!!

l'envers du décor !!...

Plumes et perles ... cajolent

le premier envol ...

!!! Jouissance !!!

De la puissance en balance !!!

Le petit Clown

en chaussons "Fourrure"

Les soupirs du tissu frémissent

et s'assouplissent !!!

71

Entre les deesse mon coeur

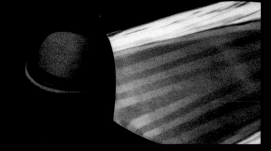

... balance ...

La vìè de Clown !

Ce n'est pas drôle !!!

La Comédie

.à l'envers !!!

La Cage d'Image

du lapin sage !!!

La terreure

du planeur !!!

!!! Pure, Souple !!!

Elle attend l'autre !!!

Savante dans son tir ,....

elle admire !!!

84

La nuit du jour

ou Chouette huit

La composition d'un

prince attendu ...

!!! *Démasquée* !!!

La reine bleue aux aveux !!!

Hiboux le jour

Chouette la nuit ...

L'Envers et le revers

... du feu ...

Dans le calme de ses entrailles,

le Clown se compose ...

Elle se dévoile de son voile

d'étoile . . .

Le réel oiseaux du chapiteau

baisse rideau :...

97

Satiné , emplumé , emperlé

chapeauté .....

Sans son masque, l'Oiseau

se meurt !!!

La fraîcheur du pinson

étincelle de sa douceur !!!

Un ange est passé ...

et rien n'a bougé ...

L'élégance de la démence

du Corps !!!

Hanté de force et désir,

le macadam soupire . . .

Le tonnerre ...

du tambour des Corps !!!

Comme les Abeilles, le Colosse

butine les fleurs du Chapiteau

Sans le voile qui l'emballe ...

la dance ne serait plus !!!!

Enlacé , attaché ,

_activé à se détacher !!!

Légère . . .

Vénus , Mars et Jupiter

La volute du

...du petit Lutin ...

De ses Rubans

elle révérence . . . . !!!

L' epervier a repit

posture

Le réveil du loup blanc

sous le décor des cordes . . .

Le lézard vert du désert, épie la terre

sans en avoir l'air !!!

Le repos bien mérité de la

guerrière envoilée !!!

une béquille !!!

"La peine

du grand Chambellan

Dans la brume, le vent

à reniflé . . .

J'ai cru te voir posé

sur ta branche !!!

Une pensée particulière

pour une dame peu ordinaire

Le raton laveur du Chapiteau

s'aventure . . .

Ensorcelée . . . .

de vie et Lumière !!!

La marche des envoilées

... s'étiole ...

Il vole de ses ailes et séduit

... de son Arc !!!

Une vague de caresse ....

s'évapore de tendresse !!!

La Colère de l'air

... sur terre ...

Comme le vent, ils sont passés ...

et repassès sans s'arrêter !!!

ACKNOWLEDGMENTS

Special thanks to the following artists from Cirque du Soleil

Chimed Ulziibayar, Elena Lev, Paul Pelletier, Tseveendorj Nomin, Vladimir Komissarov, Xavier Lamoureux, Mikhail Matorin, Georges Bertrand, Serguei Chachelev, Brian Dewhurst, Dmitro Bogatirev, Karyne Steben, Philippe Chartrand, Alexandre Zaitsev, Bianca Sapetto, Chris Lashua, Claude Chaput, Daniel Touchette, Meng Xie, Yu Wang, Quing Liu, Xiaojing Liu, Dmitro Sidorenko, Faon River Shane, Geneviève Bessette, John Gilkey, Karl Baumann, Magalie Drolet, Marie-Laure Mesnage, Olga Pikhienko, Patrick Mc Guire, Roman Polishchuk, Russel Stark, Steven Ragatz, Elena Spitsyna, Yves Décoste, Andrea Conway, Alain Gauthier, Anton Tchelnokov, Christian Paré, Francesca Gagnon, Geneviève Soucy, Gilbert Joanis, Huang Zhen, Ivan Polunin, Jean Chiasson, Leticia Carola Oliva, Martyne Dubé, France Labonté, Oleg Kantemirov, Paul-Alexandre Ahmarani, René Bazinet, Richard Lee Zumwalt, Simon Alarie, Slava Polunin, Sonya St-Martin, Vadim Bolotski.

Thank you to Guy Laliberté, Founding President of Cirque du Soleil, for writing the preface of this book. Thank you to Hélène Dufresne, Guy Laliberté and Daniel Gauthier for always welcoming me backstage at Cirque du Soleil. To Gwenael Allan for introducing me to the "Backstage." To Franco Dragone and Dominique Lemieux for creating such a visual feast. To all of the artists in their Cirque du Soleil characters who let me photograph them while rehearsing, stretching, resting, or working backstage or in the "artistic tent." Thank you to David Haley and Alain Labbé at Paris Photo Lab for their beautiful prints. Thank you to David Fahey, Fahey/Klein Gallery, who helped me put this book together.

p.11 The green lizard and
his ground woodpecker!!!

p.13 Under his hat...
...lay the feathers!!!

p.15 In the snail rings...
...the peacock fans

p.16 A bit of soul...
...Star Powder...

p.17 In the pleats and folds...
...I am twisting this body!!!

p.19 Troubador!!!
On Tour!!!

p.21 Solitary Ghost...
...Temporary Laugh

p.23 The snappy elastic
winces from innocence

p.25 He peeks...invisible
under his target

p.27 Agile!!!
The twig that points...

p.28 Island flowers
Wild birds

p.29 On the strings...
...a distant journey

p.31 From their ropes
they bewitch!!!

p.33 All these ropes will not
hold tender dreams!!

p.35 She collapses....
...collapses herself of her
rhythm.

p.36 The beautiful body
wakes up the scenery!!!

p.37 The warm-up
of a sham!!!

p.38 Roped, the needle of the
body marks time!!!

p.39 Bewitched by the ropes
she abandons herself!!!

p.41 The communion of
sweat, the chair and
the costume...

p.43 The black angel is exhil-
arated by the silence of
the day!!!

p.45 The bewitching of the
princess of the rings...

p.47 The contortion
of the peacock!!!

p.49 Enveloped by the rope
he surrenders!!!

p.51 The rope starts
its snake ritual...

p.53

One, two, three...
...ten fingers to carry
the earth!!!

p.55

The Beauty and the Beast...
...got carried away...

p.57

Relaxation for the owl...
...and knees!!!

p.59

The big nose, is better to
smell you with....my child!!!

p.61

Measure, cadence, measure
and cadence
The owls are swinging

p.62

Wild celebration of the
plumage
Flight

p.63

Warmed up, the sparrow
hawk plans his flight...

p.65

What pleasure!!!
The reverse atmosphere

p.67

Feathers and pearls...
...coax the first flight...

p.69

Pleasure!!! Of the power
in balance!!!

p.70

The little clown
in furry slippers

p.71

The fabric shivers and
sighs and becomes supple

p.73

Between the two,
my heart balances...

p.75

It's not funny
to be a clown!!!

p.77

The comedy
inside out!!!

p.79

The picture cage
of the wise rabbit!!!

p.80

The strength
of the giant...

p.81

The terror
of the glider!!!

p.83

Pure, flexible she waits
for the other one

p.84

Well-prepared for the shot...
...she admires herself

p.85

The night of the day
where the owl glows

p.87

The making of the prince
is long awaited...

p.89

Unmasked!!!
The blue queen confesses!!!

p.91

Male owl by day
Female owl by night...

p.93

The ins and outs of fire

p.94

In the calm of his being
the clown composes
himself

p.95

She unveils herself
of her star veil...

p.97

The old bird of the big top
drops curtain...

p.99

Shrouded in satin, feathers,
pearls and a hat...

p.101 Without his mask,
the bird fades away!!!

p.103 The coolness of the
chaffinch sparkles with
its softness!!!

p.105 An angel passed...
...and nothing moved

p.106 The elegance of the
insanity of the body!!!

p.107 Haunted with strength
and desire
the tarmac sighs

p.109 The thunder...
...of the body's drum!!!

p.111 Like a bee, the giant
gathers the flower nectar
of the big top

p.113 Without the veil to wrap
around herself
the dance doesn't exist!!!

p.115 Strapped, hooked
in a hurry to detach
himself!!!

p.117 Light...
Venus, Mars and Jupiter

p.118 The sensual pleasure of
the little goblin...

p.119 From her ribbons
she bows...!!!

p.121 The sparrow hawk took
back his posture...

p.123 The awakening of the
white wolf under the
decor of ropes

p.125 The green lizard of the
desert peeks at the
ground unobtrusively!!!

p.127 The well-deserved rest
of the wrapped warrior!!!

p.129 The caterpillar knits herself
a crutch!!!

p.131 The pains of the
great Chambellan

p.132 In the mist,
the wind has sniffed...

p.133 I believed I saw you posed
on your branch!!!

p.135 A particular thought
for a not-so-ordinary
woman

p.136 The raccoon of the big
top ventures out...

p.137 Bewitched...
...with life and light!!!

p.139 The walking veil...
...becomes a star...

p.141 He flies with his wings
and charms with his bow!!!

p.143 A caressing wave
evaporates itself of
tenderness!!!

p.144 The anger of the air
on earth

p.145 Like the wind, they
went... and came back
without stopping!!!

p.147 Wings

151

First Edition Published by

TONDO™

an imprint from Arena Editions

573 West San Francisco Street Santa Fe, New Mexico 87501 USA
505 986-9132 tel 505 986-9138 fax www.arenaed.com

Art Direction and Design by Elsa Kendall

Edited by David Fahey

Véronique Vial is represented by Fahey/Klein Gallery
148 N. La Brea Avenue Los Angeles, California 90036
323 934-2250 tel   323 934-4243 fax

Distribution by D.A.P./Distributed Art Publishers
155 Sixth Avenue, Second Floor New York, NY 10013
212 627-1999 tel   212 627-9484 fax

Printed by EBS, Verona - Italy

First Edition, 1999 ISBN 1-892041-10-3